Snapshots

Snapshots

Poems by

Ron Lauderbach

Cover design by Shay Culligan

ISBN: 978-1-63980-222-7

Kelsay Books
502 South 1040 East, A-119
American Fork, Utah 84003
Kelsaybooks.com

For family and friends
alive and deceased.

Acknowledgments

Thank you to the editors of the following journals for publishing my poems.

Blue Line Journal: "Catch"
The Café Review: "Chicago Winters"
The Edison Review: "Petroglyphs"
The MacGuffin: "Irvine Ranch 1960," "Lay Angel"
Mudfish Journal: "Brains," "Soap"
The Orchards Poetry Journal: "Lunch With a Friend"
Prometheus Unbound Anthology: "Entrapped"
San Diego Poetry Annual: "Animal Lover," "Lying to My
    Grandson," "Telephone Directory"
Sin Fronteras/Writers Without Borders: "It's a Job," "Smart
    Pencils"
Sky Blue Literary and Arts Magazine: "Grandpa's Alibi"
Your Daily Poem: "Pony League," "The Price of Children"

Contents

Animal Lover · 11

Irvine Ranch 1960 · 12

Grandpa's Alibi · 13

Soap · 14

The Price of Children · 15

Kevin's Sister Tells It Like It Is · 16

Death Has No Megaphone · 17

Fuller Brush Delivery Boy · 18

Pony League · 19

Moving On · 20

It's a Job · 21

Petroglyphs · 22

Telephone Directory · 23

International Dining · 24

Smart Pencils · 25

Lying to My Grandson · 26

Brains · 27

Catch · 28

Chicago Winter 2018 · 29

Dreams Can Go Viral · 30

Lay Angel · 31

Palm Sunday Vernazza 2013 · 32

Cooking Paella · 33

Entrapped · 34

Lunch With a Friend · 35

Taking My Parents to Strawberry Point · 36

Animal Lover

My grandfather loved his dogs. He cooked their food on the same gas stove he used to melt lead for bullets and make popcorn because store-bought food was not good enough and too expensive. His dogs were never allowed in the house, but he let them in the garage when it rained. Soup bones tossed into the yard kept them competitive. There were always at least a dozen chickens in the room-size cage beside his shop. Their manure was the secret of his prized red tomatoes. He named the hens but not the roosters and every spring he bought chicks he nurtured in a cardboard box he heated with a light bulb. He weighed their food and handled them as tenderly as he would an infant, until he carried them past the stump with a rusty hatchet stuck in it, to release them into the cage. His cat enjoyed evenings in the house, sleeping on my grandmother's lap, its days outside catching rodents. Grandfather was a practical man, an urban farmer, not a man of means, so when a hen stopped laying eggs or a rooster got too wild, he took it to the stump and when a dog could no longer hunt, grandfather put it in the car and said he was taking it, *to meet Mr. Remington.*

Irvine Ranch 1960

In my grandfather's '49 Dodge, seated on my holey cushion,
I nod off after eating a venison sandwich made with
homemade bread and mayonnaise, chased by a molasses

cookie with half a walnut meat in the middle, which was picked
up a couple of years before from under a tree that loved living
where the Santa Ana Freeway is now. The cattleguard rumble

wakes me as we turn off the pavement onto a dirt fire road
Frank Fitzpatrick cut with his D8 before he went home to drink
one Pabst Blue Ribbon after another, storing the empties under

his outside staircase as if they were heirlooms. Frank scraped roads
and my grandfather killed coyotes to earn hunting rights on Irvine
property. Grandfather kills the engine and all I can hear is his

a-few-days-before-a-stroke breathing and the wind. He points
at a rabbit and tells me to aim at 6 o'clock and squeeze the trigger
softly, like a cow with a sore teat. As the rifle's roar echoes then

gives up to stillness, my grandfather tells me, *That slug had
rabbit's name on it,* and I know not to answer back.

Grandpa's Alibi

I sit with Grandma in her pew. If she doesn't attend church, nobody occupies it. She is dressed up and wears a hat with a veil. The Santa Ana First Presbyterian Church has a country club feel. It is fall and many women wear stoles bearing furry fox faces with tiny glass eyes that reflect soft sanctuary lighting as do the glossy bulletins held in white-gloved hands. I can smell wool and mothballs and listen to music from a new pipe organ, donated by Glenn L. Martin, a rich aerospace engineer who is sweet on my Aunt Ruthie. From his carved, wooden pulpit, Dr. O. Scott McFarland blesses people who tithe and warns those who don't. The congregation sings hymns written by a Methodist four hundred years ago, a Methodist like the one who lives on Grandma's street, whose brother owns the Pussy Cat adult book store on Flower Street, east of 17th, near the Dew Drop Inn, that Grandpa must pass every Sunday as he drives to the dehydrator plant where he loads barrels full of hot chili peppers onto flatbed trucks driven by other men who don't attend church because they have to work on Sundays.

Soap

Exploding yellow lilies float in my
grandparents' pond. Fat goldfish
cruise the surface, bumping aquatic
plants with blunt noses as damsel
flies alight on green pads, flaunting
emerald gossamer. Pungent lye and
animal fat cooked and poured into
wooden molds surrounds the pond
and dries in the sun. Dry cakes get
chopped into chunks as hard and
rough as bricks that look and smell
so bad they can scare dirt away.
None of us kids dare swear lest
we get a mouthful.

The Price of Children

How much do kids cost? Asks my four-year-old daughter. I answer her as if she is an adult, and talk about the cost of food, shelter, and clothing. I go on to explain the importance of good heath for a better life and less medical expense. I mention family outings and entertainment, then move on to education. I think about but don't tell the emotional costs of loss of sleep, worrying, and dreaming about the future and the priceless feeling of relief when she recovered from a nearly fatal accident, last year. *Not that Daddy,* she says, *you paid when we picked up Tyler from the hospital. How much did he cost?*

Kevin's Sister Tells It Like It Is

I used to take my kids bowling in the same building that now houses Michael's and Napa Auto Parts. One block west, at the intersection of Midway and Rosecrans, there was a stand-alone building, a topless bar, its exterior plastered with the word, *Girls,* all over it. As I waited at the traffic light, to turn right onto Midway, my first-grader son read, *Girls, Girls, Girls, Girls, Girls, Girls. Daddy,* he said, *Why can't boys go in there.* His nine-year-old sister answered sternly, *They can, Kevin, and it's disgusting.*

Death Has No Megaphone

If the double-shift sawmill worker had
fastened the steel band a little tighter

If it had not rained as the flatcar rumbled
south, leaving the lumber slick and slimy

If the train crew had not humped the car on
a freezing night in the Bakersfield rail yard

If the bundle had not been forklifted from
the car five minutes before quitting time

If the lift driver had climbed off his machine
and pounded the protruding 2x4 back into place

Pappy would have retired and left the next day
for Hawaii.

Fuller Brush Delivery Boy

Newport Boulevard was a three-lane highway that connected Tustin and Newport Beach before there was a freeway. We called the middle, passing lane, the suicide lane and bragged about making it all the way down the middle. On sunny summer mornings I raced my '53 Chevrolet convertible down the middle lane, broom and mop handles jutting up from the back seat behind me, a wooden ended Tiparillo sticking out of my baby face, as I headed for the wealthiest Newport neighborhoods, to deliver domestic supplies. Before I was done for the day, I would see cowboy hats and lariats hanging on the fence that surrounded Roy Roger's and Dale Evan's tennis court. Trigger was not yet stuffed. Although I never met John Wayne, I would pull into his relatively long Lido Isle driveway, where his staff helped me unload and I could see The Duke's yacht, The Grey Goose, a converted PT boat, a cousin to JFK's PT 109. Sometimes I found Andy Devine doing his own gardening. We had a routine. I would ask him, *How's Wild Bill?* and he would hand me a dollar. I would leave Newport mid-afternoon with a pocket full of tip money and get back to Tustin in time to visit The Mad Platter and buy a couple of 45s or, on an exceptional day, an LP.

Pony League

Most boys like to go to the
white-chalked batter's box
from where they smack the
horsehide covered ball over
infielders who pivot to watch
hitters run the bases. But there
always seems to be one guy
who just can't connect. He
approaches home plate as
though it were a landmine
swings and misses or lets
the pitch fly past, while team-
mates swear and stare down
the dugout to see when they
will be up next. At his last
chance of the season, the
hitless batter, eyes closed,
swings as though he is sweep-
ing the sky and knocks a slow
roller toward the mound then
starts his half-run down the
first-baseline. The pitcher
under hands the ball to the
first baseman for the out and
the boy slinks back to the
dugout as his mother shoots
from her seat shouting, *He
hit the ball! He hit the ball!*

Moving On

My wife places a Pottery Barn Catalog order but
she will be dead before it arrives. Dr. Hauser places
a blue bottle filled with a new elixir on her stick fingers.
He says new test results will be available tomorrow,
but I know he has a standing Tuesday golf game and
while he's lying, I overhear two young nurses discuss
hospice and their social lives. Tonight will be the fourth
and possibly the last game in the World Series and
Halloween will bring trick-or-treaters. I will pick up
the kids from school, fix dinner, and help with homework.
Grieving happens when I'm by myself, in the shower or
the car. When the doctor leaves, I plop down to rest in
a hospital-hard chair and watch a sleepwalking nurse,
ten hours into a twelve-hour shift. My wife closes her
eyes then the catalog and I think about how pathetic
it is for us to put so much faith in the contents of the
blue bottle. On the way to get the kids, I call someone
I haven't talked to for over thirty years.

It's a Job

I build lumber loads—not mind-bending,
but it has to be done right. Do it faster
demands a salesman, who forgets
the load weighs seven thousand pounds,
and I have to put it together, one piece
at a time. Ten years of beers hang over
the white belt that matches his shoes. The
owner comes out and tells me to double
the short lengths end to end, and hide
them inside the load—*I have to pay for
the shorts, too,* he says. He also spends
money on martini lunches and Hawaiian
vacations I can't bury in the loads, but
they stoke my resentment. A truck driver
steps out of an air-conditioned cab, wearing
a pressed shirt, his hair slicked back like
The Fonz. He saunters around my load
with an attitude that pisses me off and
I want to punch him, but the boss is his
friend and I need to work two more years
to pay off my car.

Petroglyphs

We drive south through the toll gate
under the sunshine.
We drive south along the sand
and whitecapped sea.
We drive south past Las Playas
and the players in
Rosarito
  Ensenada
    San Quintin.
We drive south past boojum trees
that look like Dr. Seuss plants.
We drive south to Catania for
tequila and mezcal cocktails.
We drive south to Guerrero Negro
and eat birria that contains bones
too small to be from goats.
We drive east to San Ignacio
to find the church Jesuits built
300 years ago, with local people's
labor, a stone church to last
forever that most likely will
partly because of Jesuit design
but mostly due to lack of parishioners.
We drive north where we ride
horses to see drawings etched into
rocks thousands of years ago by
people who would want to keep
us out if they knew we would
leave horse manure in their caves.

Telephone Directory

I never met Otis Fudpucker
but looked up his name first
every time I received a new
phonebook and was happy
to find him listed on Otay Rd.
I mispronounced his name
a couple of times and chuckled
as I considered his childhood
challenges, then placed the tome
on a kitchen chair so my child
could eat her cheerios.

International Dining

At Panda Express I'm behind
a kid so big, I can see only
the back of his Laker's jacket.
He fills his plate and joins
his family, a worn basketball
on the seat beside him. I enjoy
watching them while I eat and
offer the kids my fortune cookie
on the way out. I think the parents
have two sons but the daughter
pulls back her hoodie, exposing
cornrows only a mother could
braid. We are in this Chinese
restaurant, as far from Sudan
as we are from China.

Smart Pencils

I keep hundreds of pencils I picked up
off the ground during my teaching career
in a PF Flyer shoebox, under my bed.
They wait for a colorful slip-on eraser
I attach when I bring one back to life.

My found pencils are not rookies from
a yellow Ticonderoga box, but
seasoned veterans, bearing bite-marks
and other scars—proof of lives lived.
Many are surprised by my electric

sharpener, a device that did not exist
when they were dropped. Some have art class
paint on them and others grease from auto-shop.
I have one that says *Oscar loves* written on
its roundness, but the name of Oscar's lover

has been sharpened away. I like to write
with my found pencils. I believe they
impart wisdom from their past lives. A lot
of pencils advertise businesses and
institutions, many of which are

gone forever. I have one pencil
with a student's name I remember
on it, in my car, in case I ever
see him around town. I have some ink
pens too, but dry—unable to reveal secrets.

Lying to My Grandson

Where do seagulls sleep?
Can you go down to the water?
How deep is it?

Wind whips my grandson's yellow
hair and makes the Golden Gate
steel-rope suspension cables sing.

Welded wire fabric stretched
along the bridge below, below railings
reminds him of the fence that

surrounds his school. *Does that keep*
animals off the bridge? Rusted blue
suicide counseling signs contrast

with orange posts. I look down and lie,
Maybe so.

Brains

Brains are vain. They all look about the same and if one has a larger frontal lobe or hippocampus than another, it is not said that one of them is more attractive. Yet the brain is the main event. Nothing human can happen without it, and I am not going to risk my brain finding out I have a different part I favor over it.

Catch

I sit with my father, looking out at the swimming pool he played in with grandchildren he no longer knows. When I tell him he should have paid me more to clean it in the sixties, he shrugs his shoulders. I pick up an Abraham Lincoln biography and notice he's on the same page he was last week. *It's interesting how Abe picked his cabinet,* I say. My father wrinkles his nose and chuckles. Setting sunlight reflects off the glass-covered photo of my father with his mixed-doubles tennis partner and sparkles in the diamonds set into the gold ring my mom insisted he buy to replace his simple wedding band, when they moved to Palm Springs. Hanging beside a letter from Ronald Reagan, he swears carries the President's wet signature, is an appreciation award from the Southern California Lumbermen's Association and an old photo of my mother wearing a bathing suit. My dad catches the ball I throw, looking at me with eyes I've never seen and slightly parted lips, his tongue flicking in and out of his mouth, like a lizard.

Chicago Winter 2018

The Uber drops us at a club where a single
incandescent bulb flickers over the name
on its door. Like in a Rod Serling scene,
I imagine it gone tomorrow, but there are
five Yelp stars and it's snowing, so we
enter and find hard seats in the back. Joe
talks to the waiter and orders a bottle of
Macallan 18. He pays with a couple of C notes
and from our new plush chairs up front, we talk
to the musicians. A trumpet player tells me
he bought his horn from Wynton Marsalis.
Me and the Macallan believe him. The next day,
by the Bean, I can't remember the name of
the club, but I can't forget that jazzed
trumpeter who loves his shiny horn with
a calligraphy *WM* engraved on the bell.

Dreams Can Go Viral

I probably shouldn't be telling you this. I should be talking to a psychologist, a priest, or maybe even the police because something is chasing me, and it means to do me harm. So far, I have no evidence, at least none that anyone would believe, but just before I wake up and immediately after, I see robot-like figures about to overtake me, throwing hand grenades filled with Covid-19. I'm hesitant to speak up. I'm afraid people will think I'm nuts but then I consider Jacob dreamed he saw angels climbing ladders to heaven about 3500 years ago, and he's still pulling that one off and Mary Shelley, while hanging out with Lord Byron a couple hundred years ago, dreamed of creating a laboratory monster and that's been good for her. Robert Louis Stevenson dreamed up *Jekyll and Hyde* and E.B. White took twenty years to develop his dream of a talking mouse into *Stuart Little*. More recently, Steven King on a flight to London, dreamed about a crazy woman who kidnapped her favorite writer and tortured him. His dream became *Misery*. So, stick around. I'm just waiting for the heavy-duty PPE I've ordered. I'll survive this and publish my thriller.

Lay Angel

Gabe hangs his shirt on the nail
that holds up his mailbox. It's a
gray day and he hopes it will dry
before he has to go to work
but he won't use his quarters
to pay for the dryer because he's
trying to save three dollars to buy
a yoyo for the kid who lives in
2B. He thinks the boy deserves it
even though he talks nasty but
more than makes up for it by
sharing his Red-Hot Cheetos with
the sick girl in 3C. The building manager,
Mrs. Martinez was Gabe's mentor.
She held rent checks and he believes
was responsible for the mysterious
appearance of food for hungry
families and other local miracles.
He knows her death has left a hole
In the angel hierarchy and prays
if he gets the promotion, it comes
with a stipend.

Palm Sunday Vernazza 2013

The man on the ladder, changing light bulbs at the church, tells us mass is at eleven. We see palm-frond icons everywhere, but they're sold out. I imagine villagers laughing at the American who cannot buy his wife this simple gift. The town turns out for the Palm Sunday procession, led by a shirtless, buff Jesus, that snakes around the commercial area to the church. The man we met on the ladder, now wearing a tie and tweed jacket, places a palm-frond cross in my wife's hand and with shimmering sky-colored eyes, before he delivers his homily says, *Buona Pasqua, Signora.*

Cooking Paella

I start small, dinner after work, a whole chicken in the crock pot with mushroom soup and veggies served on eclectic plates to a family under construction. I clear plates loaded with antipathy and passive-aggressiveness. I change the menu. Spice it up. *Carne asada a la plancha* with *mucho guacamole* and buckets of ice-cold *cerveza Mexicana*. Beer is a bad idea. At the age of seventy-one, I stir yellow paella in a pan that covers the Weber. Rice sizzles, chicken and shrimp steam in the night air. Mussels open as if to breathe. Clams smile before popping. I hope for a miracle in the saffron.

Entrapped

At lunch, my wife asks what I think about when I close my eyes as we make love. I take a bite off a fat deli pickle and sour juice drips from my chin onto sardines we bought on our honeymoon to Portugal, last year. *Isn't it rare, I say, to find containers like this, with keys that roll the lids back?* I watch the oil ooze inside the coiled cover. My wife raises an eyebrow. I imagine silver sardines bumping their nares against nylon nets.

Lunch With a Friend

Three sparrows glean the concrete floor under the table next to us. A woman strolls by with a newborn or doll bound with a Children's Hospital blanket to her chest and asks for help. We watch a girl jump off a bus and race into the restaurant and listen to the manager warn her if she is late one more time she will be fired. A young couple peruse the menu posted at the entrance, shake their heads, and walk away. A busser has a hole as big as a quarter in the sole of his sneaker. A mother with two kids checks her wallet before allowing them to order dessert. There's a 3% surcharge but nobody's wages have changed. We eat our food as we discuss line breaks, caesuras, and forms. We argue over almost everything but finally agree we both love our money.

Taking My Parents to Strawberry Point

 I bury a few scoops of their ashes at the base
of the windsock pole, beside the dirt landing

strip. My ears hear the buzz of my dad's
Cessna. I drive over to Navajo Lake where

my mom always caught the most trout and
place some ashes near their secret spot. On

the way back to their cabin, I leave a cupful
in their favorite aspen grove. At the A frame I

sprinkle a couple of handfuls around dad's stone
oven, where I smell sourdough bread. From

there I can see Strawberry Point across the valley.
Thirty minutes later, I park there, where my parents

always left their jeep, while hiking. I dig through
snow and pour some ashes where they will have

a view forever. As I slide back behind the wheel
I taste Vienna sausages and sardines. Next spring

melted snow will carry my parents to meadows
where they will live in grazing fawns and flowers.

About the Author

Ron Lauderbach writes poetry to tell stories, preserve memories, and entertain. He approaches life with a sense of humor and is happiest when his readers smile, but sometimes must be sad and serious. Ron started his professional life in the lumber business but finished as a high school English/journalism teacher. After retiring, he earned an MFA poetry at San Diego State University. He is thankful for his long life, family, and friends.

www.ingramcontent.com/pod-product-compliance
Lightning Source LLC
Chambersburg PA
CBHW030816090426
42737CB00010B/1292